Write It Right

Writing a Biography

By Cecilia Minden and Kate Roth

Published in the United States of America by
CHERRY LAKE PRESS
Ann Arbor, Michigan, 2395 South Huron Parkway, Suite 200
www.cherrylakepublishing.com

Reading Adviser: Marla Conn, MS, Ed., Literacy specialist, Read-Ability, Inc.
Book Designer: Felicia Macheske
Character Illustrator: Carol Herring

Photo Credits: © Katya Shut/Shutterstock.com, 5; © wavebreakmedia/Shutterstock.com, 7; © Erickson Stock/Shutterstock.com, 11; © Waraporn Chokchaiworarat/Shutterstock.com, 13; © YAKOBCHUK VIACHESLAV/Shutterstock.com, 15

Graphics Throughout: © simple surface/Shutterstock.com; © Mix3r/Shutterstock.com; © Artefficient/Shutterstock.com; © lemony/Shutterstock.com; © Svetolk/Shutterstock.com; © EV-DA/Shutterstock.com; © briddy/Shutterstock.com; © IreneArt/Shutterstock.com

Library of Congress Cataloging-in-Publication Data

Names: Minden, Cecilia, author. | Roth, Kate, author. | Herring, Carol, illustrator.
Title: Writing a biography / by Cecilia Minden and Kate Roth ; illustrated by Carol Herring.
Description: Ann Arbor, Michigan : Cherry Lake Publishing, 2020. | Series: Write it right | Includes bibliographical references and index. | Audience: Grades 2-3
Identifiers: LCCN 2019033384 | ISBN 9781534158993 (hardcover) | ISBN 9781534161290 (paperback) | ISBN 9781534160149 (pdf) | ISBN 9781534162440 (ebook)
Subjects: LCSH: Biography as a literary form—Juvenile literature.
Classification: LCC CT21 .M55 2020 | DDC 809/.93592–dc23
LC record available at https://lccn.loc.gov/2019033384

Cherry Lake Publishing would like to acknowledge the work of the Partnership for 21st Century Learning, a Network of Battelle for Kids. Please visit *www.battelleforkids.org/networks/p21* for more information.

Printed in the United States of America
Corporate Graphics

CHERRY LAKE PRESS

Table of

CONTENTS

CHAPTER ONE

What Are Biographies?

Have you ever read a **biography**? Biographies help us learn about the lives of real people. They can be about famous people, such as sports stars, artists, or world leaders. They can also be about regular people. Everyone has a story to tell.

You can write a biography about someone you know!

Here's what you'll need to complete the activities in this book:

- Blank notebook paper
- Pencil with an eraser
- Computer (optional)

You will need to gather your materials.

Some biographies are better than fiction!

CHAPTER TWO

Everyone Has a Story

Who do you want to write about? The subject of your biography does not have to be famous. They don't even have to be an adult. Think about the people in your life. You might want to learn more about a friend, coach, grandparent, neighbor, or person at your school. Pick someone of interest to you. You may be surprised by what you learn about the people you see every day!

You need to do **research** to write a good biography.

ACTIVITY

Make a List

In this activity, you will make a list of possible subjects for your biography.

INSTRUCTIONS:

1. Make a list of people you would like to write a biography on.
2. Choose someone who is interesting to you.

Sample Planning Sheet

SUBJECTS FOR MY BIOGRAPHY

- Aunt Alice, an artist ✓
- Grandpa Nick, who can build anything
- Hope, my friend who collects bugs

When a person writes their own story, it is called an autobiography.

CHAPTER THREE

Did You Know?

Once you choose who to write about, you can decide what you want to learn about that person. Now it's time to do more research! Sometimes you can get the information you need from a book or on the computer. For this biography, you will do research to learn about your subject with an **interview**.

Your questions should help you find out more information about your subject. Where were they born? What was it like growing up? Ask what they like to do and what places they like to visit. If the person is older, you can move on to questions about their life as an adult. What are their greatest **accomplishments**? What would they like others to know about them?

ACTIVITY

Prepare to Interview Your Subject

In this activity, you will prepare the questions for your interview.

INSTRUCTIONS:

1. Write the title "What I Know" at the top of the page.
2. List the facts you already know about your subject's life.
3. On a second page, write the title "What I Want to Know."
4. List what you want to learn from the interview.
5. On a third page, write the title "Questions."
6. Write your ideas for questions to ask your subject. Your notes about what you want to learn can help you think of questions.
7. Leave space under each question to write down the person's answers.

Sample Activity: MY AUNT ALICE

WHAT I KNOW

- She always liked to draw and sketch.
- She went to college to study art.
- She likes to work with paint.
- She volunteers teaching art classes.

WHAT I WANT TO KNOW

- Where she went to school.
- Why she chose painting.
- What inspires her ideas.
- When she started volunteering.

QUESTIONS

- Where did you study art?
- How did you get started in painting?
- Where do you get your ideas?
- When did you start volunteering?

Friends or family can give you background information on the subject of your biography.

CHAPTER FOUR

The Interview

Call or write the person to set up a time for your interview. Make sure you allow plenty of time to ask your questions. You don't want to rush the interview. It is a good idea to use a recording device during the interview. That way, when it's time to start writing, you'll be able to review what was said. A smartphone will allow you to record an interview.

Look at the person while they are talking. Be a good listener. Follow your list of questions. Other questions may come up during the interview. Keep good notes on what was said.

Interview Your Subject

In this activity, you will interview the subject of your biography.

INSTRUCTIONS:

1. Turn on the recording device if you are using one. Don't forget to turn it off after the interview is over.
2. Ask the questions on your list. Give the speaker time to answer each one.
3. Listen carefully. Take notes on what you want to remember about each answer. Your notes do not have to be full sentences, but they should be clear so you can understand them later.
4. Look at the speaker as you ask your questions.
5. After the interview, thank the person for taking time to talk with you.

Always ask permission before you record an interview.

Sample Activity

Q: Where did you study art?

A: I studied at the Kansas City Art Institute. I took many classes to learn all types of art.

Q: How did you get started in painting?

A: As a kid, I always liked to draw and sketch in my journals. I discovered acrylic paint when I was studying and loved all the colors. And I still draw in my journals!

Q: Where do you get your ideas?

A: Artists see shapes, colors, and designs in everything they see. I get ideas from nature, people, and life.

Q: When did you start volunteering?

A: I've been volunteering as an art teacher for the past 2 years. It is my way of helping children to see their potential as artists.

Always use good manners, and be polite during an interview.

CHAPTER FIVE

Step By Step

Now you are ready to write a **draft** of your biography. Choose which information you want to use from your notes. You do not have to use everything you learned. Think about what **adjectives** you can use to describe this person and his or her life. Write what is important or interesting about your subject. What makes them unique? Help the reader see the person as you do.

Biographies are often written in **chronological** order. This means you write events in the order they happened. You should also organize the information into **categories**. Categories are sections with information on one topic. For example, your first category might be the subject of growing up. Next, you might write about events in the person's life. Finally, you could write about the person's special accomplishments.

Use **quotations** from your interview. When you quote someone, you must write exactly what he or she said. Using quotations will allow your readers to hear your subject's voice.

Organized notes will make it easier to write your biography.

ACTIVITY

Create a Draft

In this activity, you will write a draft of your biography.

INSTRUCTIONS:

1. Choose the information you want to use from your research.
2. Add a title to your biography.
3. Write an opening statement to grab the reader's attention.
4. Put the information in chronological order.
5. Divide the information into categories. Each category will form a **paragraph** in the body of the biography.

MY AUNT ALICE, AN AMAZING ARTIST

INTRODUCTION

If you ever go to the Larchmont Gallery, you will see many beautiful paintings. In the lower right-hand corner of each painting is the name of the artist, Alice. I know her as Aunt Alice, and she is an amazing artist.

FAMILY AND HOME LIFE

Aunt Alice was the youngest of four daughters. My mom, Ann, is the oldest. Alice always liked to draw and sketch. She went to college to learn how to create many kinds of art. It was there she discovered her love of painting.

FAVORITE ACTIVITIES

Aunt Alice travels all over the world. She gets many ideas from her trips to France and Italy. She always brings me really cool surprises, too. She has a studio in her home where she does her work. It has big windows. Aunt Alice said it is important to have lots of natural light when creating art.

PAYING IT FORWARD

Two years ago, Aunt Alice was asked to teach an art class at the YMCA for its after-school program. Now she teaches twice a week and a 6-week course in the summer. She likes working with students and encouraging them to try new things. I took a class with Aunt Alice last summer. It was so much fun. I think I would like to be an artist when I grow up, just like my Aunt Alice.

CHAPTER SIX

Introducing

After you finish your draft, go over your work. Make changes until everything is just right. Write your final copy on a blank sheet of paper or type it using a computer.

Biographies often contain pictures of the subject. Find photographs or draw illustrations to go with your writing.

You can take your own photos to include in your biography.

ACTIVITY

Final Changes

Check everything one more time.

- Do I have a title and opening that will grab the reader's attention?
- Do I help the reader get to know the biography's subject?
- Do I use words that explain the chronology of events?
- Do I include details that help give the reader a clearer picture of the person?
- Is the information organized into categories with headings?
- Do I have an illustration or photograph of the subject?
- Do I use correct grammar and spelling?

Share your biography with your subject and with others. Let others learn about your subject's unique life!

GLOSSARY

accomplishments (uh-KAHM-plish-muhnts) important things a person has done in his or her life

adjectives (AJ-ik-tivz) words used to describe nouns

biography (bye-AH-gruh-fee) a book telling the story of a person's life

categories (KAT-uh-gor-eez) similar ideas grouped together

chronological (krah-nuh-LAH-jih-kuhl) arranged in the order in which events happened

draft (DRAFT) an early version of a written document

interview (IN-tur-vyoo) a meeting during which a person is asked questions about themselves or a subject

paragraph (PAR-uh-graf) a group of sentences about a certain idea or subject

quotations (kwoh-TAY-shuhnz) sentences or short passages that are written or spoken by one person and repeated by another

research (REE-surch) a study or investigation into a particular subject

For More
INFORMATION

BOOKS

Fletcher, Ralph. *How to Write Your Life Story.* New York, NY: Collins, 2007.

WEBSITES

Ralph Fletcher
www.ralphfletcher.com/tips.html
Get some great writing tips from a famous author!

INDEX

About the AUTHORS

Cecilia Minden is the former director of the Language and Literacy Program at Harvard Graduate School of Education. She earned her doctorate from the University of Virginia. While at Harvard, Dr. Minden also taught several writing courses. Her research focused on early literacy skills and developing phonics curriculums. She is now a literacy consultant and the author of over 200 books for children. Dr. Minden lives with her family in McKinney, Texas. She enjoys helping students become interested in reading and writing.

Kate Roth has a doctorate from Harvard University in language and literacy and a master's degree from Columbia University Teachers College in curriculum and teaching. Her work focuses on writing instruction in the primary grades. She has taught kindergarten, first grade, and Reading Recovery. She has also instructed hundreds of teachers from around the world in early literacy practices. She lived with her husband and three children in China for many years, and now they live in Connecticut.